My Night in the Planetarium

by Innosanto Nagara

When I was seven, I got to spend the night in a planetarium.

This is a true story. Do you want to hear it?

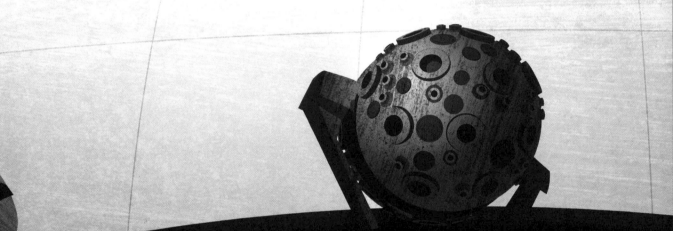

I was born in Indonesia.

Only three countries in the world have more people
than Indonesia. Do you know what they are?

China. India. The United States. Then comes Indonesia.

Indonesia is an ARCHIPELAGO, which means it's made up of lots of islands.
There are SEVENTEEN THOUSAND islands in Indonesia. There are 300
different ethnic groups. People speak 750 different languages and dialects.

Indonesia is rich in natural resources. Fish from the sea. Fruit from the trees. And spices.

Ooh, the spices.

Indonesia is where the Spice Islands are. When you learn about Columbus, you will learn that he was looking for the Spice Islands when he got lost and was shipwrecked in Haiti. But that's another story.

Let's get back to Indonesia. People from all over the world came to Indonesia to buy spices. Some of them, like the Dutch, decided to stay.

We Indonesians are really nice, so we let them stay.

They stayed for 350 years.

Finally, Indonesians decided it was time for the Dutch to go home. They hadn't been very good guests. They stole our spices. They took over our government. And they put people in jail if they complained.

So people from all across the Indonesian islands decided to UNITE and kick them out.

We called this **The Indonesian Revolution.**

After the revolution we all lived happily ever after. **The End.**

No, not really. This is a true story, so things are more complicated than that.

Just before I was born, a new ruler came to power. He was
a general from the military, and was used to everyone
following his orders. He ruled Indonesia with
an IRON FIST. Lots of people were afraid
of him. He let his family and friends get
rich, while the rest of the country was
poor. And just like the Dutch, his
army put people in jail if they
complained.

My dad, who you would call *Datuk* in Indonesia, is a poet and a playwright. He and his friends would gather for poetry readings. And he had a theater troupe that put on plays that lots of people would come to watch.

Datuk and his theater troupe believed in Free Speech and didn't think that the General was treating people well. So they decided to do a play about how that was wrong. They put up posters all over town and they called the play *Ssst!*

That's Indonesian for "Hush!" or "Be quiet!" or . . . well, you probably know other, ruder ways to tell someone you want them to stop speaking, don't you?

The theater troupe would rehearse their play in our garage every day. I would hang out and listen. Because I was seven, and a good listener, I was able to memorize the whole play. When the actors would forget their lines, I would remind them.

I think this annoyed them a bit, so they finally said, hey, if you're going to be so good at remembering all these lines you should be in the play. So my dad made a part for me. I got to be a spy.

The play was really popular. Lots of people came to see it, because they'd heard it was a clever play. It was a story about people who were being ruled by an evil king from another land. But the people united and kicked out the king. There were many heroes, but one hero in particular stood out and became their new leader. But then that new leader started acting like the old king—letting his family get rich and putting people in jail who complained.

Everyone knew the play was about the General, but since it didn't ACTUALLY say it was about him, they hoped they wouldn't get into trouble.

Our family traveled across Indonesia with the theater troupe performing the play. Everywhere the play went, more and more people came to see it. At the same time, people across Indonesia were protesting against the General. University students were protesting in the streets. Poets were reading protest poems. And folk singers were singing protest songs.

Some of them were arrested for saying what they really thought.

That's when we heard that the General was really mad. He'd ordered his soldiers to arrest my dad and the other actors. The soldiers were going to come after the play closed and the audience had gone home.

So that night everyone in my dad's theater troupe brought their toothbrushes to the performance. They figured, well, if you're going to go to jail for a long time, you may as well have your toothbrush with you so you can keep your teeth clean.

(true story)

The performance was in a huge theater complex called TIM. There were indoor stages, outdoor stages, a movie theater, and even a planetarium. During the week, I took Balinese dance lessons in one of the smaller theaters.

Since my dad's play
was really popular,
they were performing it
in the BIGGEST outdoor
theater.

The final performance was a
success. But sure enough, after the
audience left, the soldiers came to
find my dad.

And yet, he was nowhere to be found! The theater was empty. My dad and all the actors had snuck out with the audience. My mom and I had said goodbye to him as he got into a *bajaj** in the alley behind the theater. Then he headed out of town to lay low for a while.

The problem was, we couldn't go home either because we heard that the soldiers were waiting at our house. That's when my mom said, let's go to the planetarium!

So my mom and I went to the planetarium
and watched the show. Then we watched it
again. And again.

It was dark and beautiful under the stars.

And we were safe.

I fell asleep on my mother's lap.

And THAT is how I got to spend the night
in the planetarium.

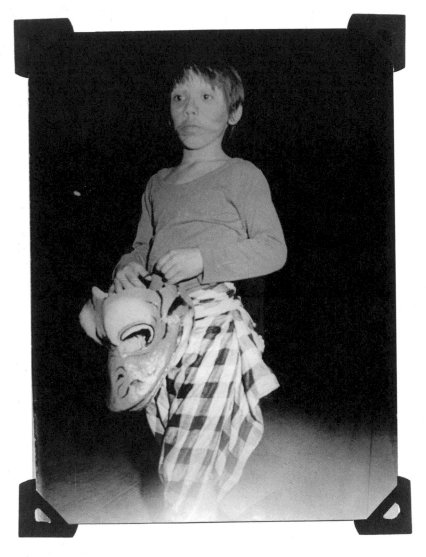

This is me when I was eight in my dad's play *Rimba Tiwikrama* (The Jungle Is Furious), an environmental play against the logging companies. I got to be a frog.

Epilogue

I hope you enjoyed my story. I know some of it might have seemed a bit scary for a kid. But honestly, it wasn't scary for me at the time. I knew my family would take good care of me.

Datuk stayed away for a while, but then came back and did many other plays. I got to be in some of those plays too. Everyone thought I was going to grow up to be an actor. But I decided I wanted to study biology. And now I'm an activist and a graphic artist. It's okay to change your mind about what you want to be when you grow up.

This is my dad wearing a mask in a two-hour solo play called *Zaman Topeng* (The Era of the Mask), which he performed in many countries, including the United States.

Meanwhile, my dad continued to do new things too. He did cutting-edge solo plays (those are plays where he was the only actor in them), he got to read his poetry on national TV, he ran for parliament, and is now a famous movie star. He has won many awards, including Indonesia's equivalent to an Oscar.

The General ended up ruling Indonesia for over thirty years. He was finally forced to step down in 1998 after massive demonstrations across the country led by students. Some time after that, the General died.

That's my dad, in the middle, starring in a 2013 movie for which he received a Best Actor award.

Notes

Datuk is what you call someone who is an elder or in particular your grandfather. *Mbah* is what I called my grandmother.

T.I.M. is short for *Taman Ismail Marzuki*. Ismail Marzuki was a famous Indonesian composer. We just called the art center TIM.

A *bajaj* (pronounced bah-jai) is a small three-wheeled "taxi" of sorts that is very common in Indonesia.

Dedicated to Arief Romero & his mama, Kristi

Special thanks to Sacha, Jupi, Jaiah, Marcos, Lucia, Arief, Amil, Amado, Mayari, Mico, Joaquin, Kavi, Silar, Ila, Theo, Emma, William, Sam, Tossan, Aiko, Mabel, Ena, Anna, Eva, Helen, Miguel, Henrietta, Clementine, and all the other kids and parents who test-drove this book and shared your insights and critical feedback.

Thank you also to Ruth Weiner and Veronica Liu at Seven Stories for recognizing the book in this story. And of course to Dan Simon for having the foresight and vision to know this existed long before I did, and for encouraging me to write it.

Seven Stories Press
140 Watts Street
New York, NY 10013
www.sevenstories.com

Library of Congress Cataloging-in-Publication Data – TK

Printed in the United States.

DATE DUE

MAR 0 3 2020